CW00349782

Easy Living

with Captain Cuddlepuss

First published 2004 by Pan Macmillan Ltd
Pan Macmillan, 20 New Wharf Road, London N1 9RR
Basingstoke and Oxford
Associated companies throughout the world
www.panmacmillan.com

ISBN 0 7522 1569 8

Produced under license by Aardman Animations © and ™ Aardman Ltd 2004

Text © Pan Macmillan Ltd 2004

2 4 6 8 9 7 5 3 1

A CIP catalogue record for this book is available from the British Library.

Design by Dan Newman @ Perfect Bound Ltd
Text by Natalie Jerome

Colour Reproduction by Aylesbury Studios Ltd.

Printed by Proost, Belgium

'Cats can appear to be lazy but I don't think they are.'

captain cuddlepuss

spanner & trousers

'I like seeing friends and just sort of, taking it easy and being comfortable.'

'I think
Feng Shui should
be introduced to
all office
environments.'

primrose

"The icing on the cake would be the partner or companion who would be there with me for the next number of years."

'Cats just sit about all day and get fed.'

captain cuddlepuss

'You can leave a cat to it.'

'I like just sitting down, eating, drinking and being merry.'

K & C SKIPS

fergal

'I find the sound of the sea really, really peaceful.'

'The cat
just walks around
with his tail
in the air.'

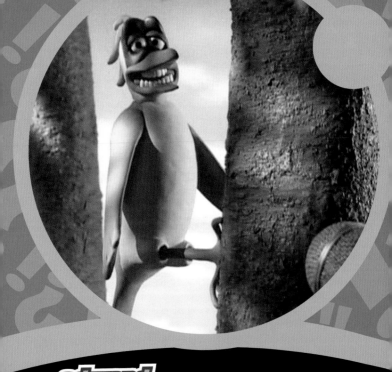

edward

"Well, a garden is a place for contemplation isn't it? For reflection."

fluffy

'I love sunbathing because its very warm and its very relaxing and its almost like being in bed really isn't it? It's like having a big electric blanket all the time.'

'The ideal weather for me is dry, about 68. 65 to 68 I'm perfect. Anything over that or under that I'm struggling. Especially in cold mornings, I shouldn't really go out in cold mornings, I shouldn't go out in the wind and also, I should y'know, do what I can do. I say some days I can move mountains, the next day I can't do anything.'

flat fish

'I've been under a lot of pressure lately.'

'I think cats make good pets.'

captain cuddlepuss

clement

'I'm nicely happy in my life now, having been took off the shelf, and it's a nice family that I'm in now and that's a very nice, comfortable, sort of feeling.'

'We're definitely –
what would you say? – gourmets
or gourmands, whichever word it
is. We like to indulge and enjoy
food really. And I think
probably there's a good variety in
what we eat – Thai, Indian,
Chinese, French, Italian,
traditional British.
As long as it tastes good,
I'll eat it really.'

'Cats just sit, they can sleep for so long.'

'I'm certainly a loyal companion but I have to say that I've been let down a lot too in my life. I might be very loyal and like my father said before me, he said "You trust everybody once," and that's what I do, I trust everybody once no matter who they are. So I'm loyal...to the point of disloyalty.'

pickles

'I'm not a cat person, they don't do anything, they just wee all over the garden and leave brown stains all over the grass.'

'I'm alright walking
on the flat, and downhill, but
I can't go uphill. As soon as
I start to go uphill I get chest
pains, it starts to tighten up
but what I do, where I live,
there's a downhill slope, down
to what they call the Co-op,
I walk down there and come
back on the bus.'

pickles

'You may as well enjoy life because you don't live for very long. I like to enjoy life.'

'You can't
be morbid.
You've got to
have a laugh
and a joke,
y'know.'